Colorful File Folder Games

Carson-Dellosa Publishing Company, Inc.
Greensboro, North Carolina

GRADE
K

Table of Contents

Credits

Author: Debra Olson Pressnall
Editors: Donna Walkush, Caroline Davis, Jennifer Taylor
Layout Design: Mark Conrad
Art Project Coordinator: Julie Kinlaw
Inside Illustrations: Bill Neville, Bill Lunsford, Ray Lambert
Cover Design: Annette Hollister-Papp
Cover Illustration: J. J. Rudisill

ISBN 0-88724-269-3

Introduction

General Instructions

Materials Needed for Each Game:
- letter-size file folder
- poster board
- resealable plastic bag
- scissors
- glue, rubber cement, or spray adhesive
- lamination film or clear contact paper (optional)

Directions:
1. For each game, remove the game board pages. Glue the pages to a file folder, overlapping them to complete the scene. Note: Due to the printing process, the game board panels may not align precisely. If needed, trim off part of the border.
2. Cut out the game label and glue it to the tab on the file folder.
3. Cut out the game instructions and glue them to the front of the folder.
4. Glue the game cards, game pieces, and answer key to poster board. Then, cut them out.
5. Laminate the game folder, game pieces, and answer key or cover with clear contact paper for durability.
6. On the back of each file folder, attach a resealable plastic bag to make a storage pocket for the game pieces and answer key.

Additional Suggestions:
You may wish to code the game pieces, for example, by writing the game title's initials on the back of each piece. Or, color code each game. For example, glue the game board to a yellow file folder and glue the game cards, game pieces, and answer key to yellow poster board. These methods will quickly identify the game to which a misplaced piece should be returned.

Directions for each game include icons to help students read the directions. Review what each icon means (below) and review all directions with students before letting them play the games.

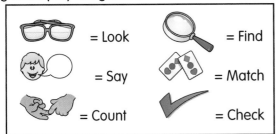

= Look	= Find
= Say	= Match
= Count	= Check

Language Arts Games

Leaping Letters

Skills: To identify beginning consonant sounds; to match beginning sounds to letters

Special Instructions: For game 1, remove the lily pad picture cards and let students use the frog letter cards. For game 2, remove the frog letter cards and have students match the lily pad picture cards to the pictures on the game board.

Space Race

Skills: To identify uppercase and lowercase letters; to match uppercase and lowercase letters

Icy Treats

Skills: To identify matching colors; to identify color words; to match colors and color words

Special Instructions: For game 1, use the ice cream topping cards and remove the color word cards. For game 2, use the color word cards and remove the ice cream topping cards.

Ollie Octopus with Opposites

Skills: To identify opposites; to match words that are opposites

Sledding Fun

Skill: To identify rhyming words; to match rhyming words

Pouch Pals

Skill: To identify rhyming words; to match groups of rhyming words

Special Instructions: After laminating the game board, create a pouch on each kangaroo by cutting along the dashed line with a craft knife. Have students slide the game cards into the pouches. The game cards can also be placed around or on top of each kangaroo.

Under the Big Top

Skill: To identify rhyming words; to match pairs of rhyming words

Clowning Around

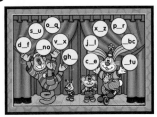

Skill: To identify lowercase letters; to put groups of letters in sequential order

Math Games

Counting Cats

Skills: To count sets of objects up to nine; to identify numbers, number words, and number sets; to match numbers to number sets; to match number sets to number words; to match number sets to number sets

Special Instructions: For game 2, the number word cards or the number set cards can be removed to match students' skill levels.

Patterns on Paths

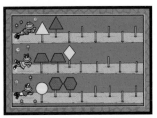

Skill: To identify shapes in patterns; to determine the correct order of shapes needed to complete patterns

Catch That Number

Skills: To identify numbers, number words, and number sets; to match numbers and number words; to match number sets and number words; to count sets of objects up to 10

Special Instructions: For game 1, remove the number set cards. For game 2, remove the number cards.

Bunches of Bananas

Skill: To count objects; to recognize numbers in sets of five; to count objects in groups of five

Banking Coins

Skill: To recognize pennies, nickels, and dimes; to count coin values up to 20¢; to match sets of coins to money values; to understand the values of a penny, a nickel, and a dime

Special Instructions: For game 1, remove the money bag cards. For game 2, remove the coin cards.

Flower Patch Patterns

Skills: To identify shapes; to recognize patterns; to complete shape patterns

Shipshape Math

Skills: To identify shapes; to recognize objects as shapes

Classy Sorting

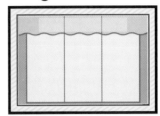

Skills: To group objects by color and category

Special Instructions: For game 1, include the game piece labeled "Type." For game 2, include the game piece labeled "Color."

Balloon Lineup

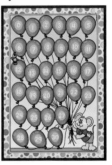

Skills: To identify and correctly sequence numbers 0-30

Counting on Candy

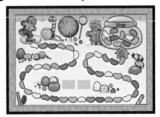

Skills: To add two sets of objects; to recall addition facts up to 10

Special Instructions: Explain to students that two people are needed to play the game. Instruct each player to choose a game marker. Explain that the yellow and white cards should be placed facedown in separate piles on the two blue boxes on the game board. Instruct players to take turns drawing a card from each pile, then adding the jelly beans. Have each player move his game piece ahead the number of spaces that matches the answer.

Directions

Game 1:

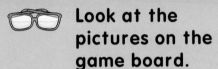 Look at the pictures on the game board.

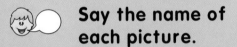 Say the name of each picture.

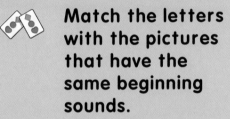 Match the letters with the pictures that have the same beginning sounds.

✔ Check your work.

Game 2:

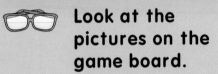 Look at the pictures on the game board.

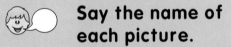 Say the name of each picture.

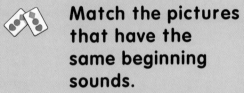 Match the pictures that have the same beginning sounds.

✔ Check your work.

Leaping Letters
Answer Key

Game 1:

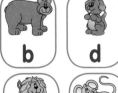 b   d   f   h   k

 l   m   n p r

 s   t   v z

Game 2:

    q

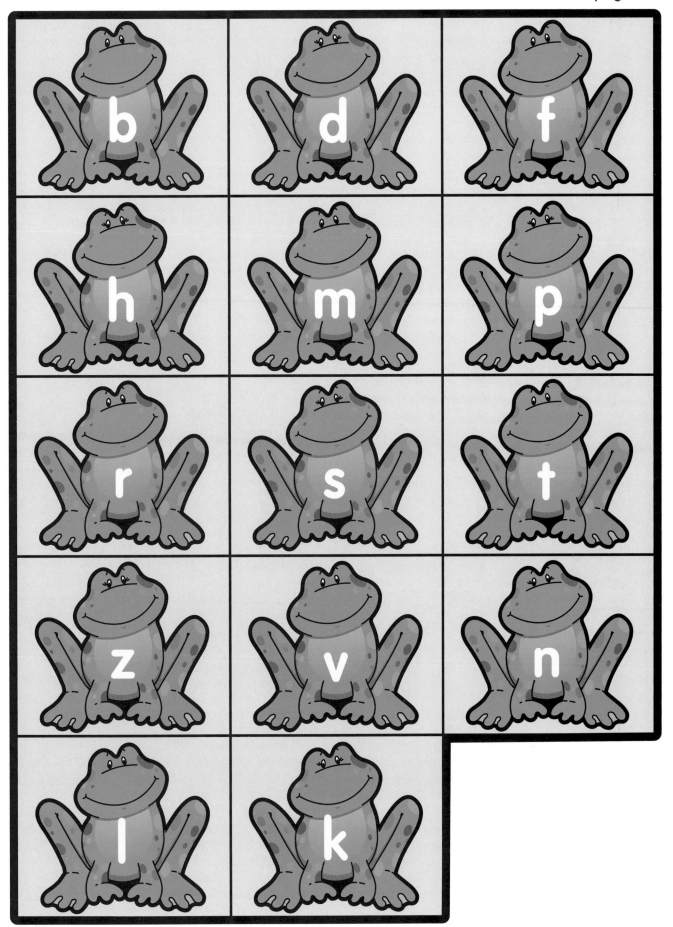

CD-104048 *Colorful File Folder Games*

Space Race

Directions

- Look at the letters on the game board.
- Look at the letters on the game cards.
- Say the names of the letters.
- Match the uppercase and lowercase letters.
- Check your work.

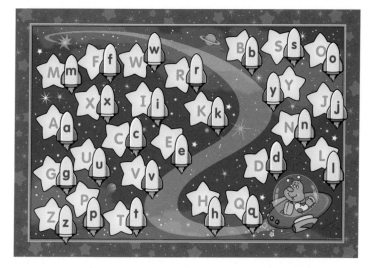

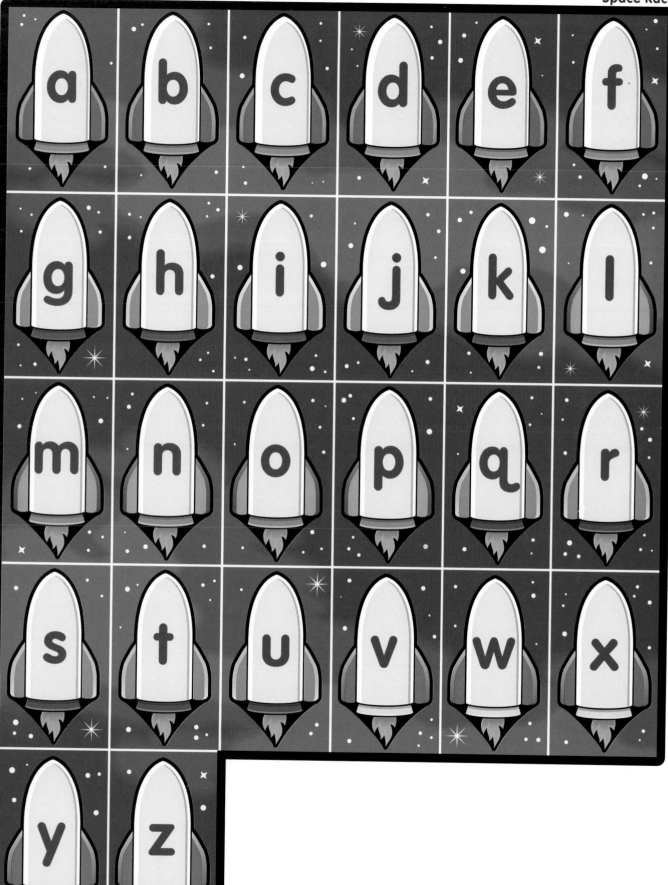

CD-104048 *Colorful File Folder Games*

Directions

 Look at the pictures on the game board.

 Look at the pictures on the game cards.

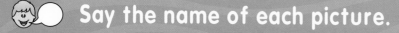 Say the name of each picture.

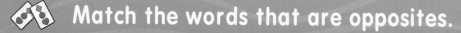 Match the words that are opposites.

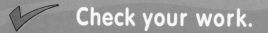 Check your work.

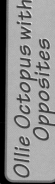

Ollie Octopus with Opposites

✔ Ollie Octopus with Opposites
Answer Key

hot — cold   over — under   day — night

sad — happy   dirty — clean   in — out   big — little

open — closed   right — left   back — front

over

back

dirty

open

sad

in

right

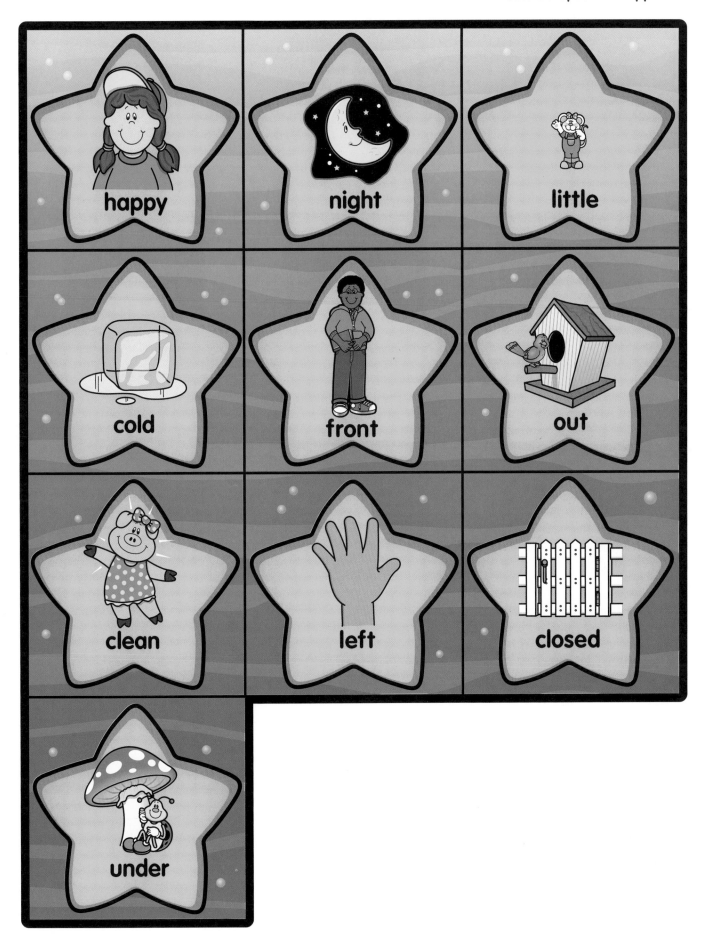

happy

night

little

cold

front

out

clean

left

closed

under

22

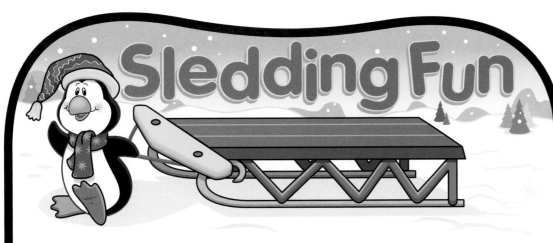

Directions

 Look at the pictures on the game board.

 Look at the pictures on the game cards.

 Say the name of each picture.

 Match the words that rhyme.

Check your work.

 Sledding Fun
Answer Key

sled

men

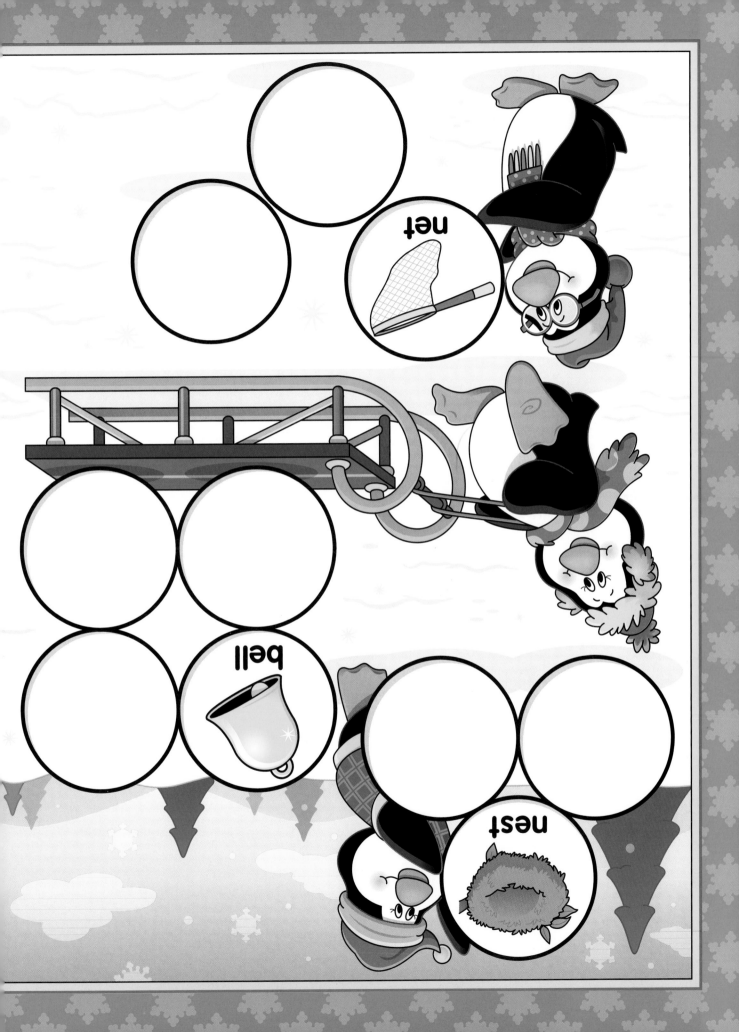

net

bell

nest

Pouch Pals

Directions

Look at the pictures on the game board.

Look at the pictures on the game cards.

Say the name of each picture.

Match the words that rhyme.

Check your work.

Pouch Pals

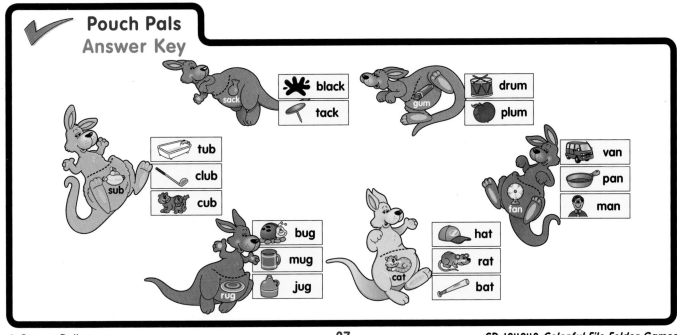

Pouch Pals
Answer Key

sack — black, tack

gum — drum, plum

sub — tub, club, cub

van — pan, man

bug — mug, jug (rug)

hat — rat, bat (cat)

gum

cat

fan

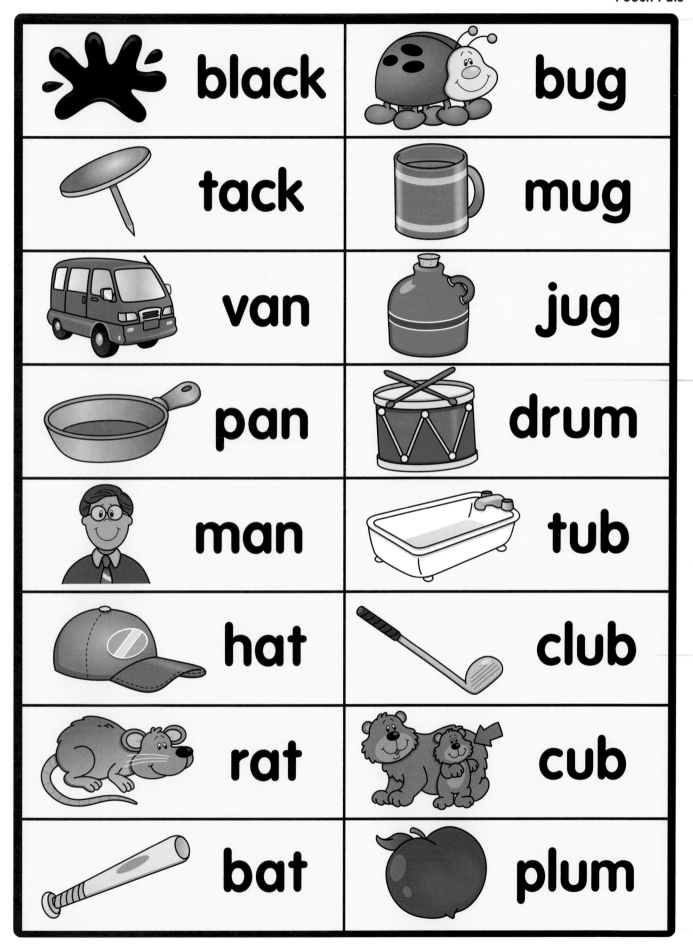

black

bug

tack

mug

van

jug

pan

drum

man

tub

hat

club

rat

cub

bat

plum

Directions

 Look at the pictures on the game board.

 Look at the pictures on the game cards.

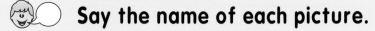 Say the name of each picture.

 Match the words that rhyme.

✔ Check your work.

Under the Big Top
Answer Key

crib | bib

king | ring | ship | lip

chick | brick | pig | wig

fish | dish

frog | log

clock | lock | top | stop

pot | cot | fox | box

Bob | cob

frog

clock

top

pot

fox

cob

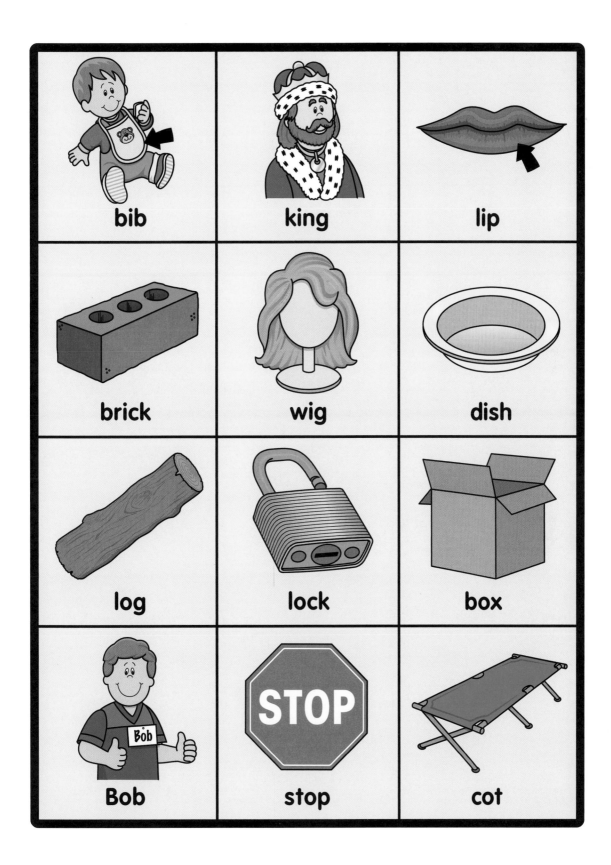

bib

king

lip

brick

wig

dish

log

lock

box

Bob

stop

cot

34

Directions

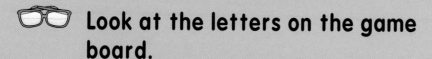 Look at the letters on the game board.

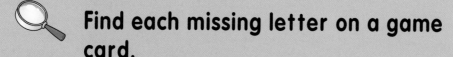 Find each missing letter on a game card.

Match each game card to the game board.

Check your work.

Clowning Around Answer Key

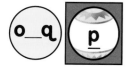   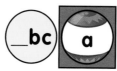

o_q p v_x w _bc a x_z y

s_u t _no m c_e d p_r q

 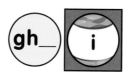 

d_f e gh_ i _tu s j_l k

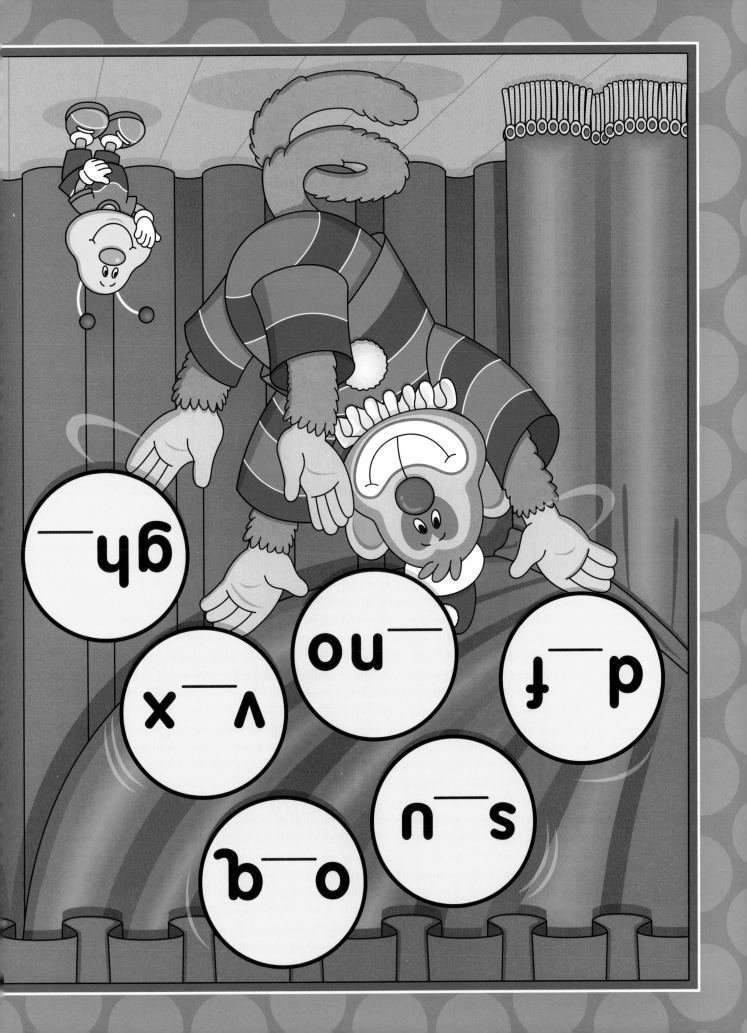

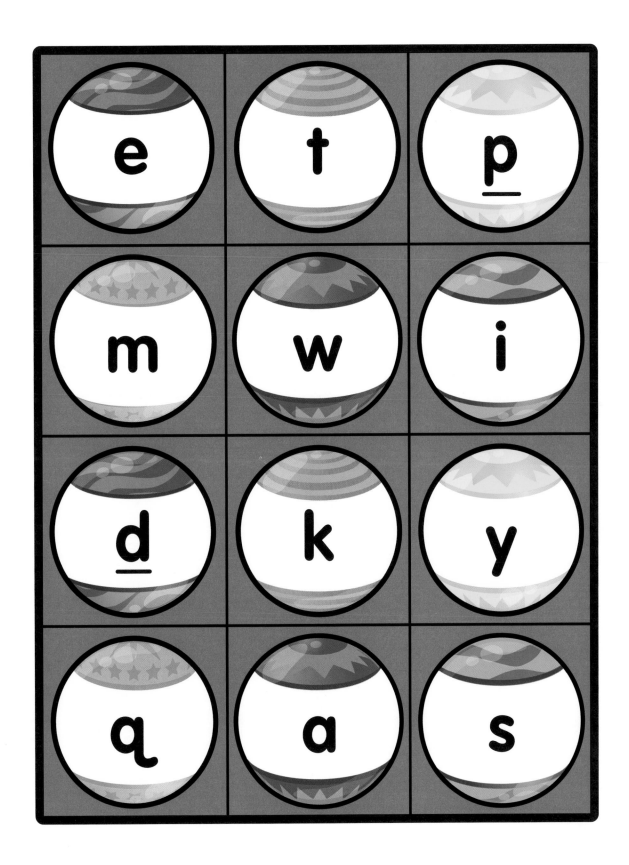

Directions

Game 1:

 Count the cats with each hat.

 Match the correct pink card to each group of cats.

 Check your work.

Game 2:

 Count the cats with each hat.

 Match the correct blue card to each group of cats.

 Match the correct yellow card to each group of cats.

 Check your work.

Counting Cats

Counting Cats Answer Key

Game 1:

Game 2:

1	2	3	4	5
6	7	8	9	one
two	three	four	five	six
seven	eight	nine		

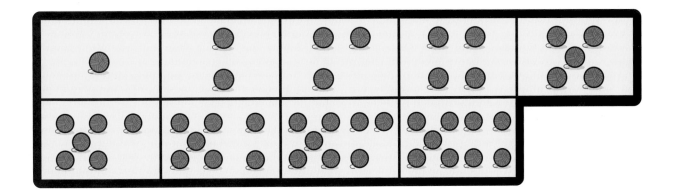

Directions

Game I:

 Look at the shapes on the game board.

Use the game cards to finish the patterns.

 Check your work.

Patterns on Paths

Patterns on Paths
Answer Key

Game I:

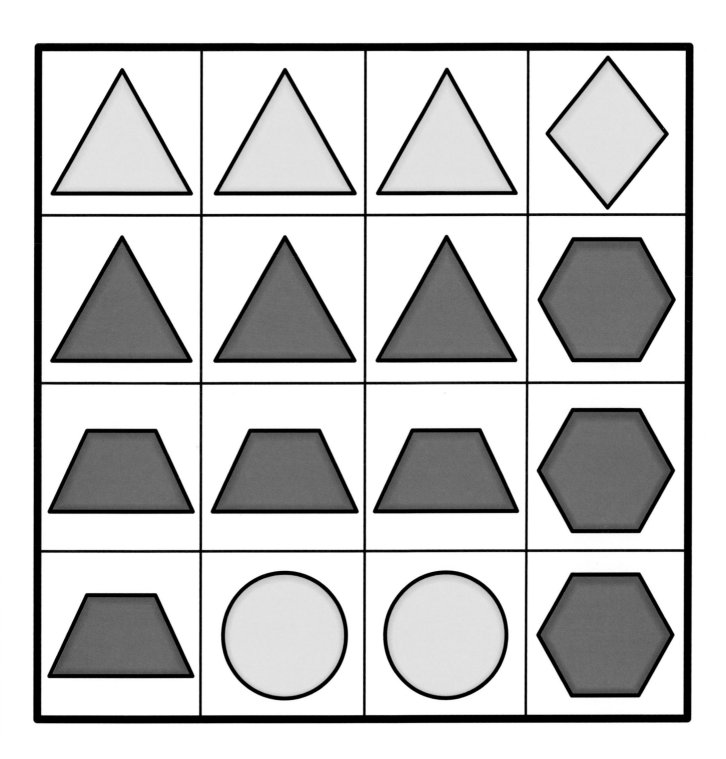

Directions

Game 1:

 Look at the number words on the game board.

 Match the number cards to the correct number words.

 Check your work.

Game 2:

 Look at the number words on the game board.

 Count the dots on each baseball card.

 Match each set of dots to the correct number word.

 Check your work.

Catch That Number
Answer Key

Game 1:

Game 2:

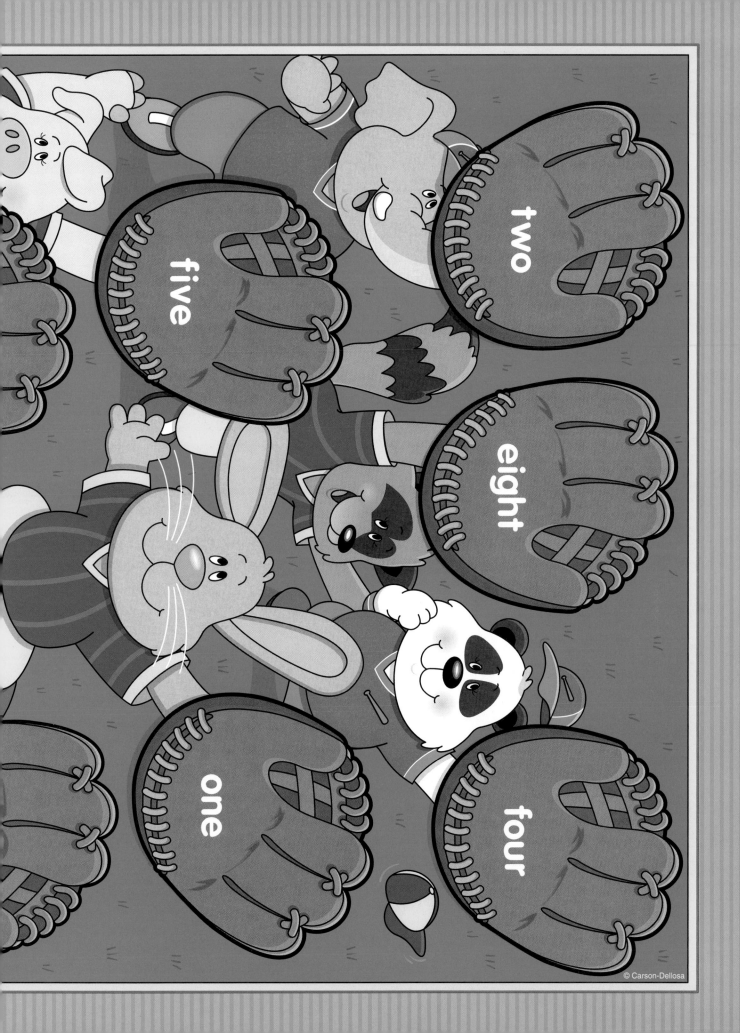

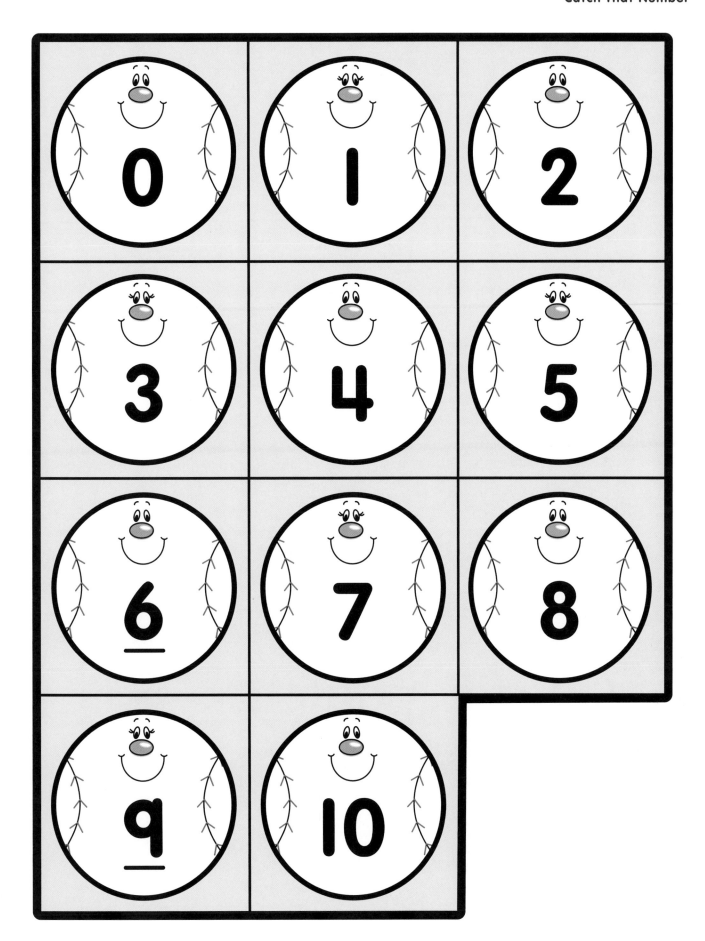

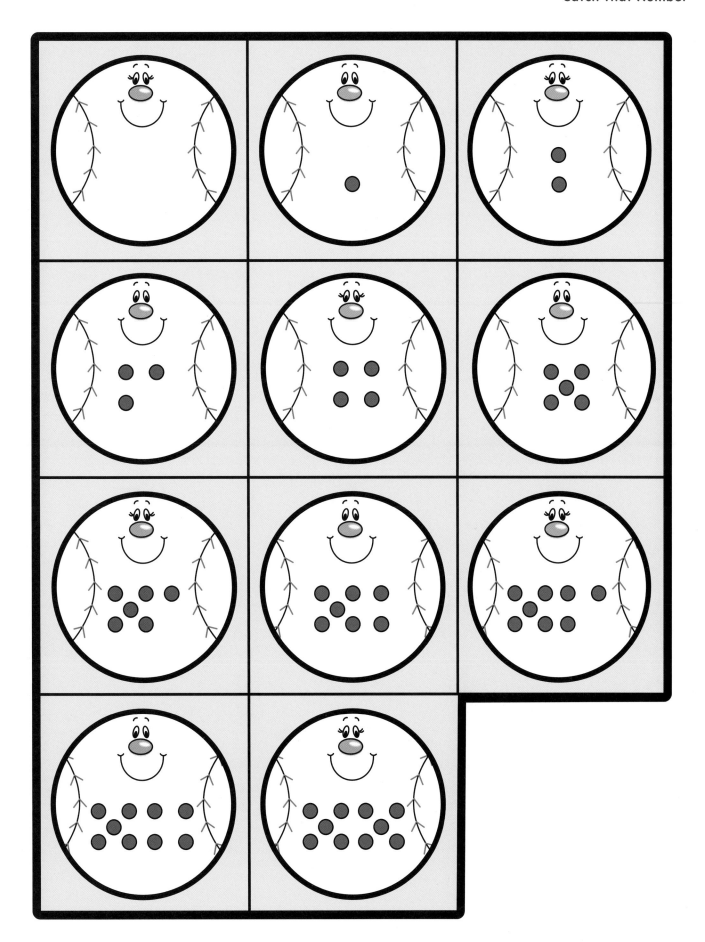

Directions

 Look at the numbers on the game board.

Put the correct number of bananas in each basket.

 Check your work.

 Bunches of Bananas
Answer Key

CD-104048 *Colorful File Folder Games*

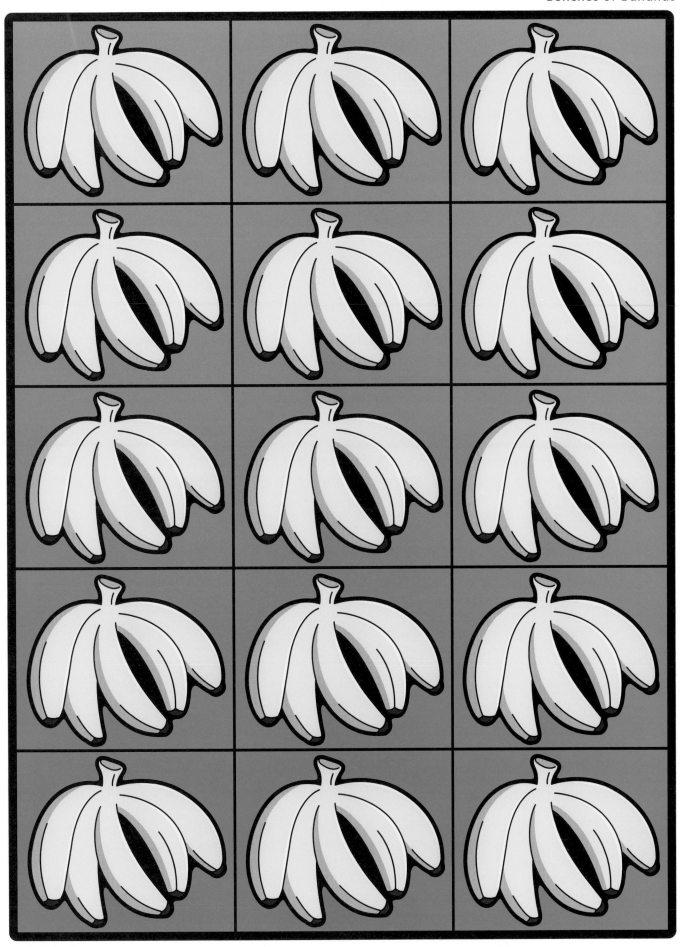

CD-104048 *Colorful File Folder Games*

Banking Coins

Directions

Game 1:

Look at the numbers on the piggy banks.

Count the coins to match the number on each piggy bank.

Check your work.

Game 2:

Look at the numbers on the piggy banks.

Match the money bags to the correct piggy banks.

Check your work.

Banking Coins

Banking Coins
Answer Key

Game 1:

 8¢ =

 10¢ =

 14¢ =

15¢ =

20¢ =

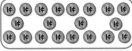

Game 2:

 8¢ =

 10¢ =

14¢ =

 15¢ =

20¢ =

CD-104048 *Colorful File Folder Games*

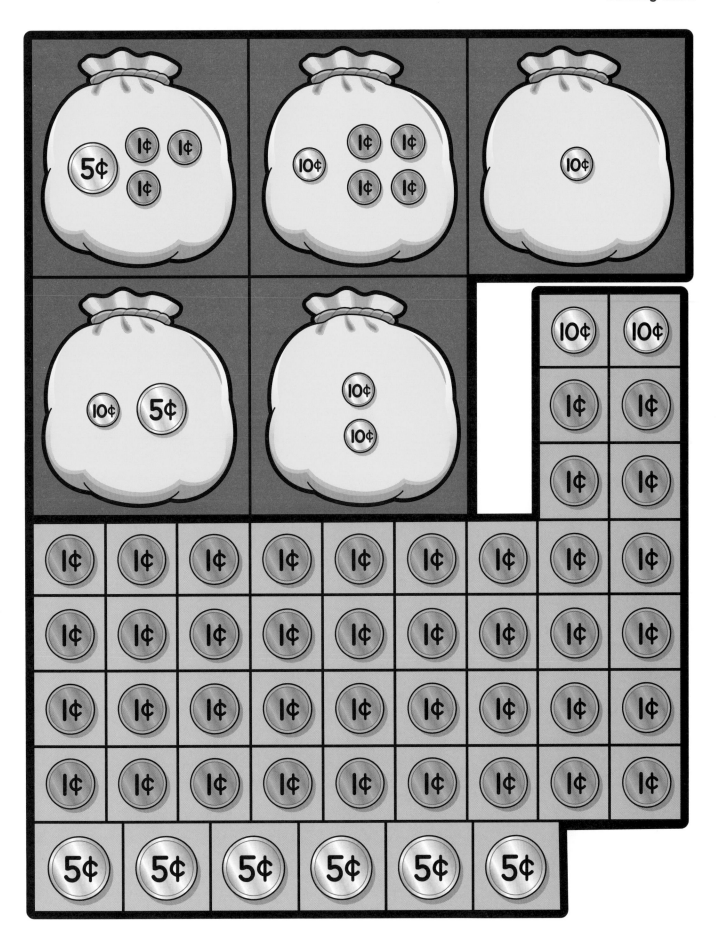

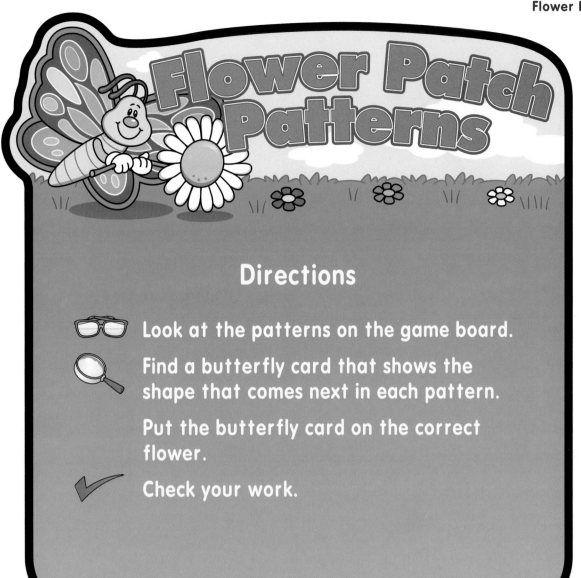

Directions

Look at the patterns on the game board.

Find a butterfly card that shows the shape that comes next in each pattern.

Put the butterfly card on the correct flower.

Check your work.

Flower Patch Patterns

Flower Patch Patterns Answer Key

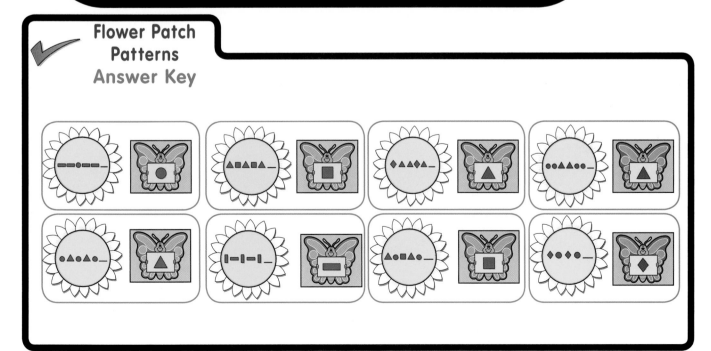

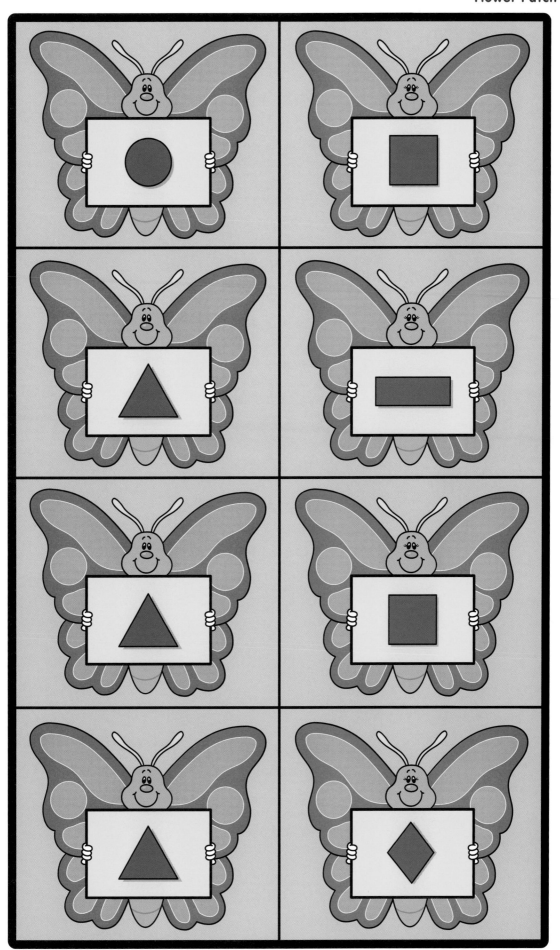

CD-104048 *Colorful File Folder Games*

Directions

 Look at the shapes on the game board.

 Look at the pictures on the game cards.

 Match the shapes and pictures that are the same.

 Check your work.

Shipshape Math

 Shipshape Math
Answer Key

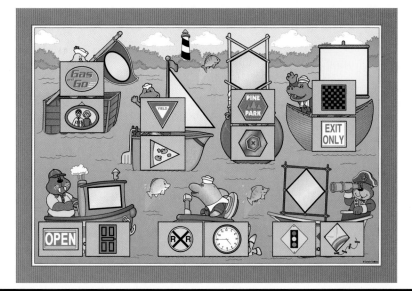

hexagon

square

circle

rhombus

Directions

Game 1:

Place the Type card at the top of the game board.

Look at the picture cards.

Sort the pictures into groups of pets, toys, and shapes on the game board.

Check your work.

Game 2:

Place the Color card at the top of the game board.

Look at the colors on the game cards.

Sort the game cards by color on the game board.

Check your work.

Classy Sorting
Answer Key

Game 1:

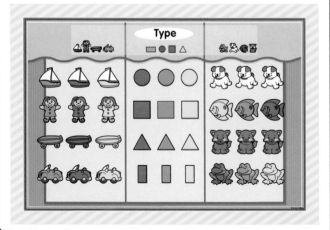

Game 2:

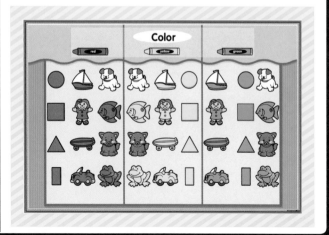

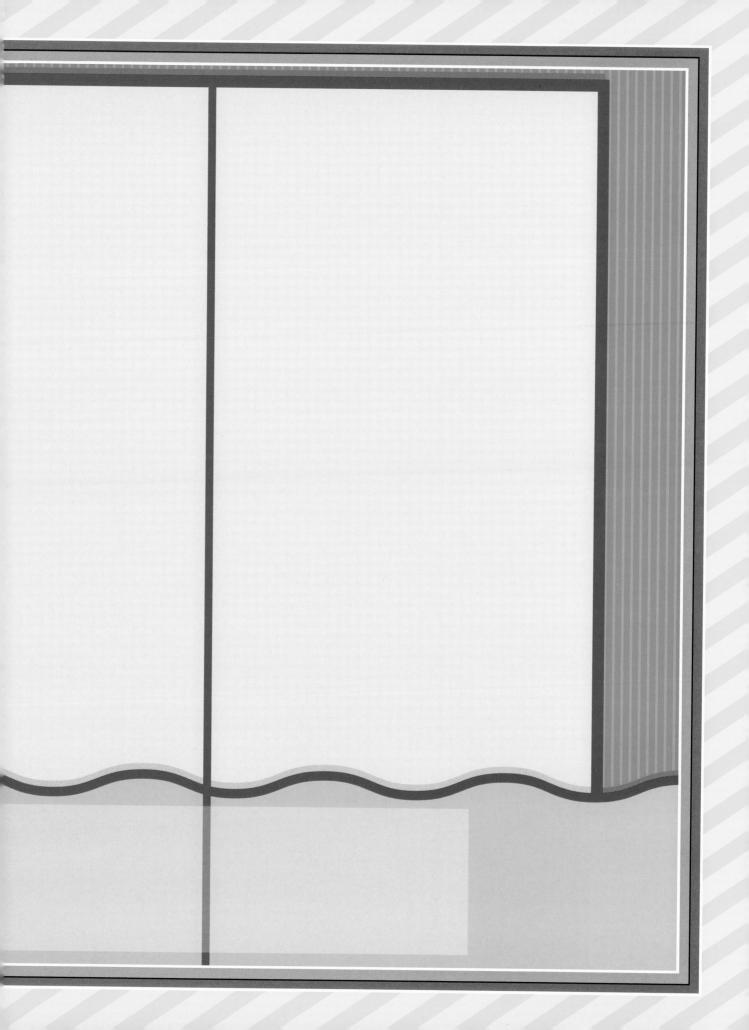

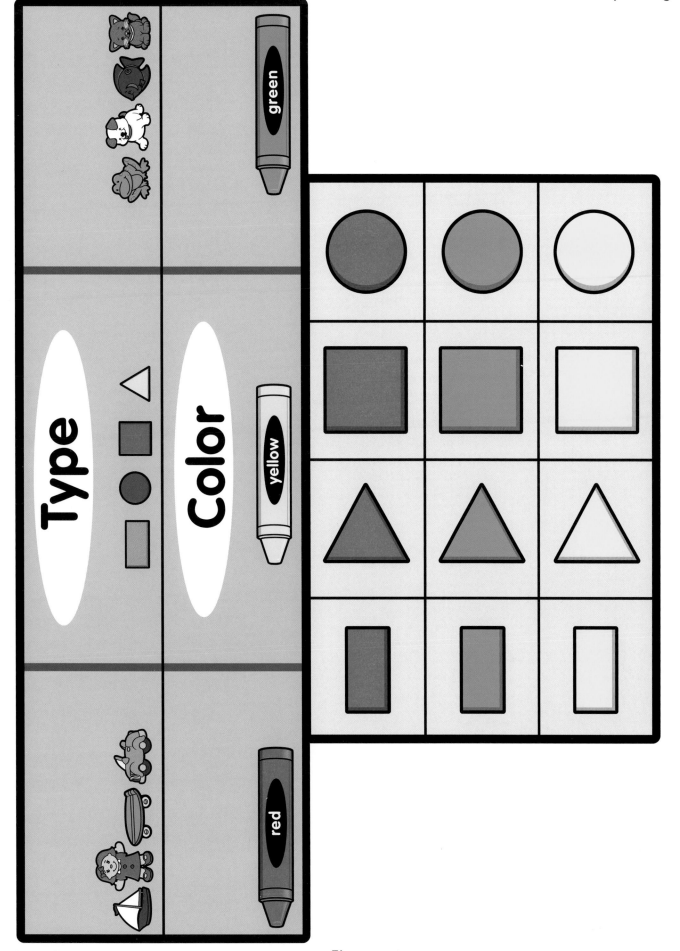

72

Directions

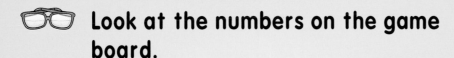 Look at the numbers on the game board.

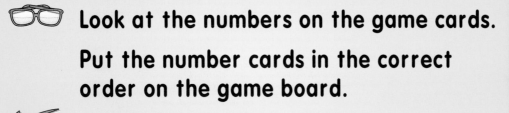 Look at the numbers on the game cards.

Put the number cards in the correct order on the game board.

✔ Check your work.

✔ **Balloon Lineup**
Answer Key

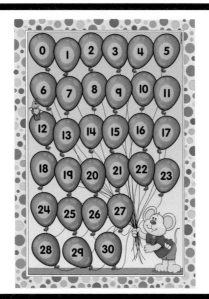

0	1	2	3	4	5
<u>6</u>	7	8	<u>9</u>	10	11
12	13	14	15	16	17
18	19	20	21	22	23
24	25	26	27	28	29
30					

CD-104048 *Colorful File Folder Games*

Directions

Ask a friend to play with you.

Pick a game piece.

Put the yellow cards in one pile.

Put the white cards in another pile.

Pick a card from each pile.

Add the jelly beans together.

Move your game piece the same number of spaces as your answer.

Play until a player reaches "Stop."

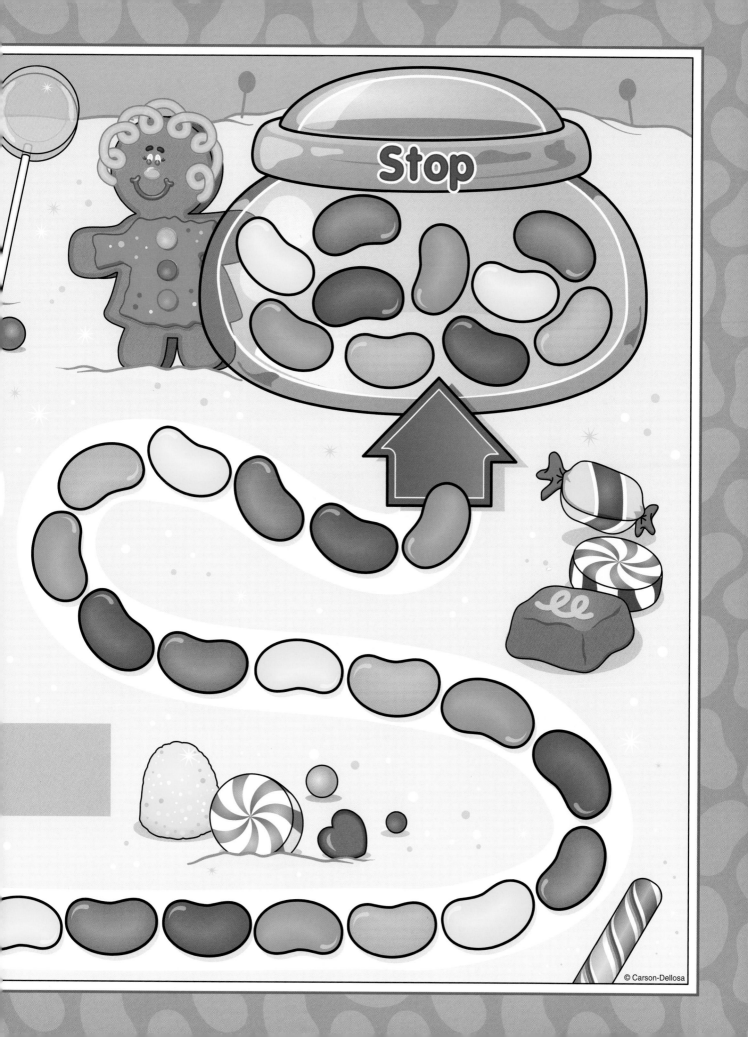

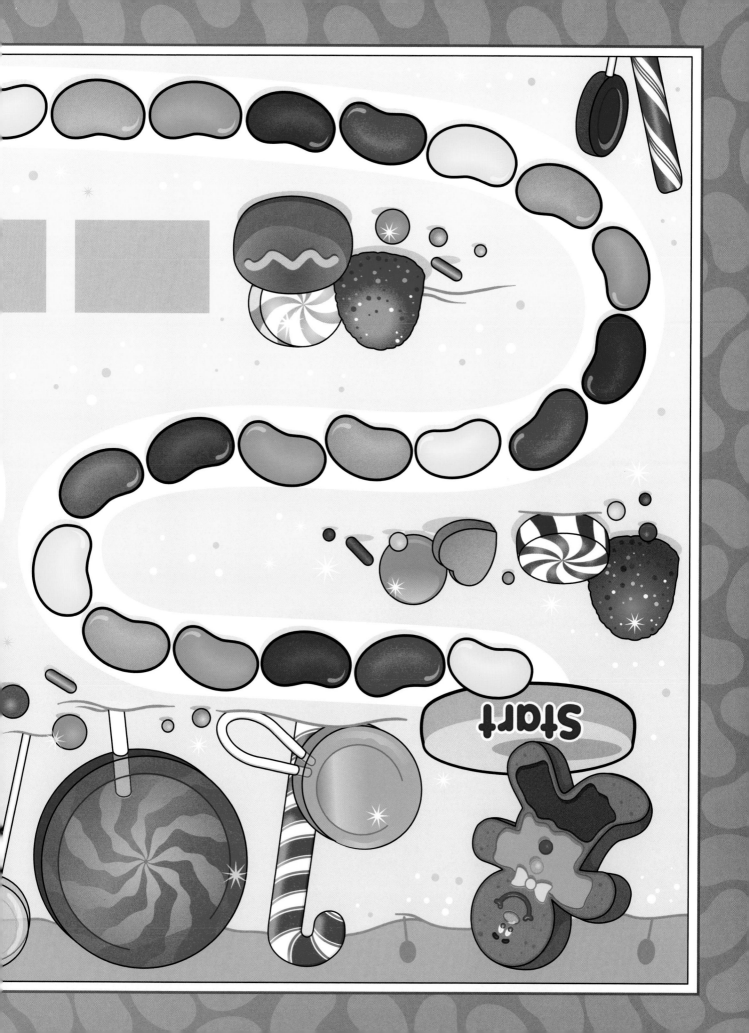

Start

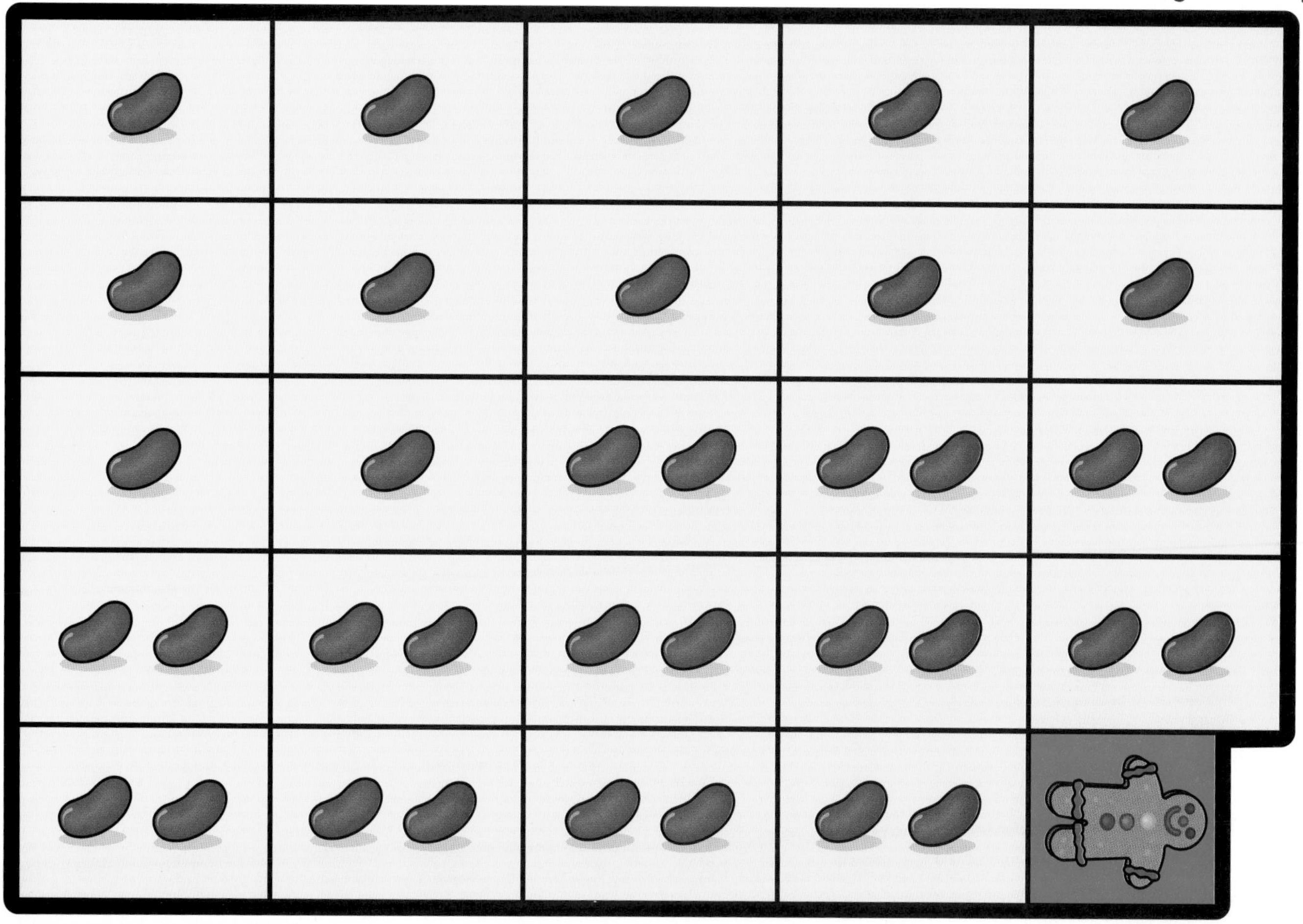

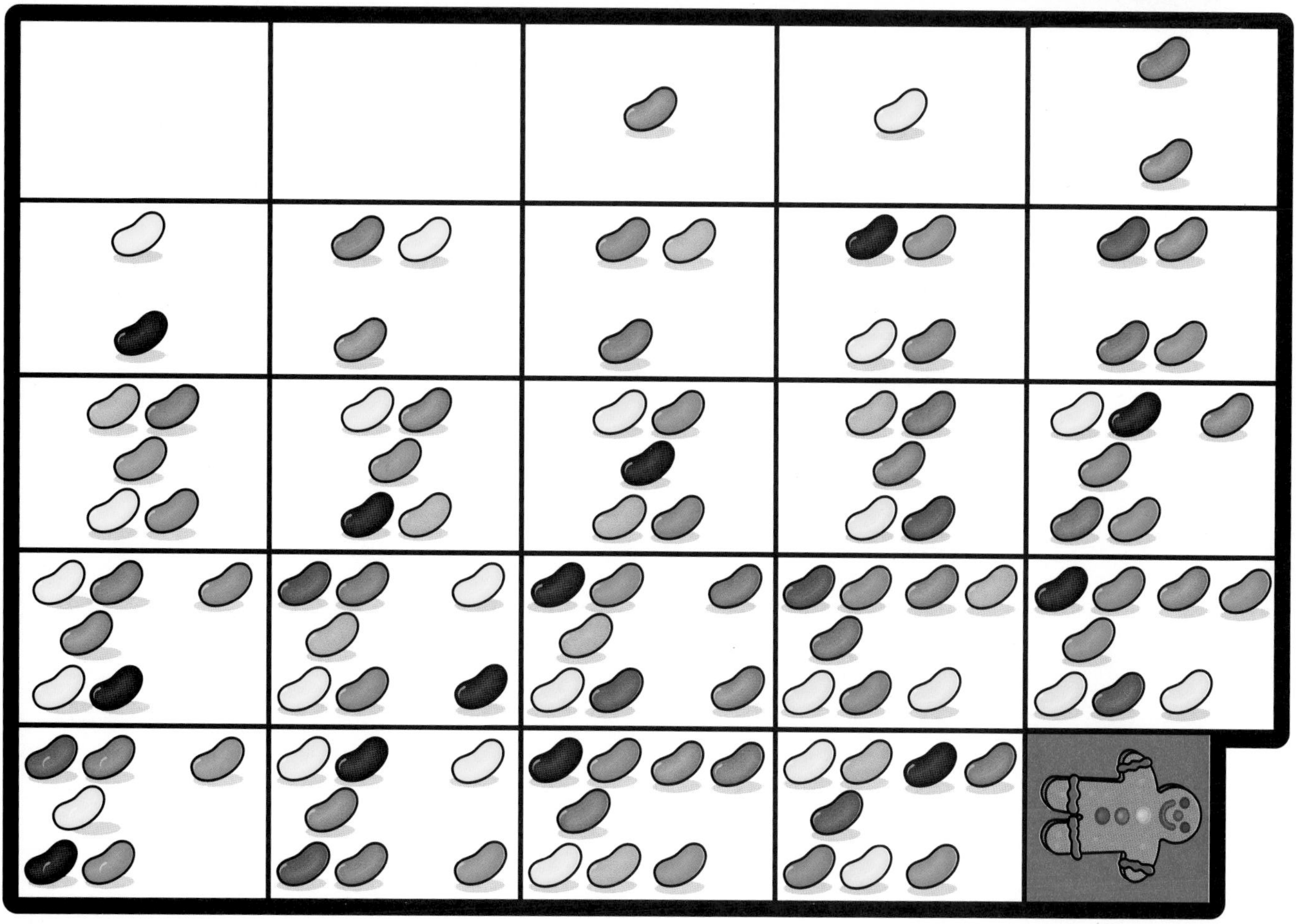